The Conflict Resolution Library™

Dealing with Being the Youngest Child in Your Family

• Elizabeth Vogel •

The Rosen Publishing Group's
PowerKids Press™
New York

To J.T. — for being the youngest, too.

Published in 2000 by The Rosen Publishing Group, Inc.
29 East 21st Street, New York, NY 10010

Photo Credits: Cover, pp. 4, 12 © Skjold Photographs; pp. 7, 15, 19 © 1992 Gazelle Technologies Inc.; pp. 8, 11, 20 © Ira Fox; p. 16 © Seth Dinnerman.

First Edition

Layout and design: Erin McKenna

Vogel, Elizabeth.
    Dealing with being the youngest child in your family / by Elizabeth Vogel.
        p.   cm. — (The conflict resolution library)
    Includes index.
    Summary: Describes some of the frustrations and benefits that come with being the youngest child in a family and offers advice on how to deal with both.
    ISBN 0-8239-5407-2 (lib.bdg.)
    1. Birth order—Psychological aspects—Juvenile literature. 2. Youngest child—Psychology—Juvenile literature. 3. Sibling rivalry—Juvenile literature.
[1. Birth order. 2. Brothers and sisters.]   I. Title. II. Series.
    BF723.B5V65 1998
    155.9'24—dc21   98-46438
                                                                                    CIP
                                                                                    AC

Manufactured in the United States of America

Contents

The Youngest Child

Are you the youngest child in your family? If so, you have at least one older brother or sister. Maybe you have even more than one. As the last child born, you have an important place in your family. Being the youngest can be very special. You may get lots of attention from your family members. Your family may love taking care of you. However, being the youngest can also be **difficult**. You are not always allowed to do the same things as your older brothers and sisters. This can be **frustrating**.

◀ *Older sisters or brothers can be there for you in good times and bad times.*

Siblings

You're lucky, you have a **sibling**. A sibling is a brother or sister. Your siblings might even look like you. Having siblings can be fun. You almost always have someone to play with you. You can cheer each other up when one of you feels sad. As you and your siblings grow up, you will learn a lot from one another. You can count on your siblings to be there for you. You will feel good knowing that you are there for your siblings, too. Sometimes a sibling can even be your best friend.

Sisters and brothers are not only in the same family, they can be good friends, too. ▶

Having Trouble

Brothers and sisters don't always get along. Sometimes you might **argue** with your siblings. This is because you disagree about something and get angry. Maybe your sibling has said something that upsets you. You might feel like your older sibling is being bossy. Tell her how you feel. Try to figure out if you can **compromise**. This means both of you try to give in a little. A compromise would be reached by sharing the last cookie with your sister. It's good to find a way for everyone to be happy.

◀ *If you disagree with your sibling, talking it out is the best way to try to solve the problem.*

Michael and Tonya

Michael was playing with his toy helicopter in the living room. "You can't play in here!" his older sister, Tonya, cried. "Go play somewhere else." Sometimes Tonya felt she could tell her brother what to do because he was younger, but Michael knew he was allowed to play there. Michael said, "I am allowed to be here, Tonya, and I don't like it when you boss me around." Even though Tonya was older, Michael knew she shouldn't try to boss him around.

Sometimes older siblings might try to boss you around. It can be helpful to tell them how this makes you feel. ▶

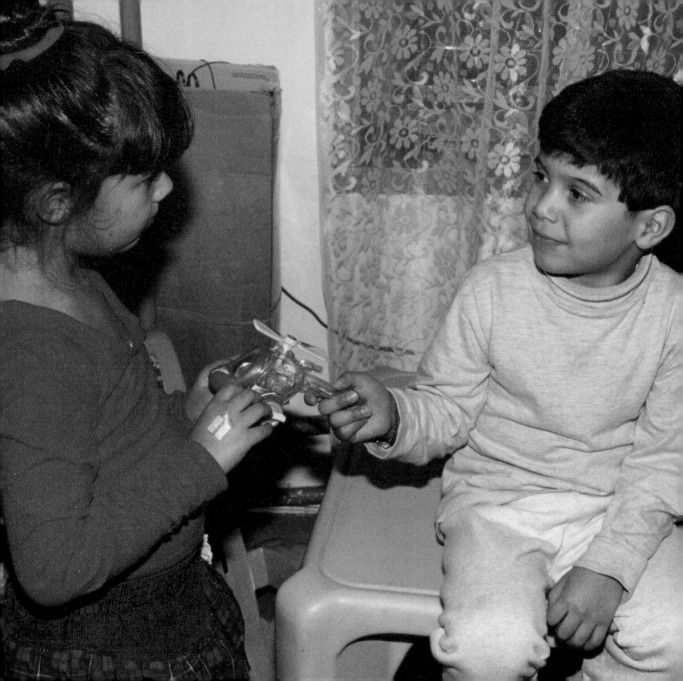

I Want to Grow Up

Younger siblings often want to grow up just as quickly as their older siblings. However, they aren't always allowed to do the same things because they are younger. Does your brother have a later bedtime than you do? Is your sister allowed to go to the park with her friends, but you are not? Maybe you wish you could wear her cool clothes. Waiting until you are older to do special things can be upsetting and seem unfair. Try to enjoy the fun things you love to do right now.

◀ *Sometimes the baby in the family wants to be like an older sibling. Always remember just to be yourself.*

Cathy and Ellie

Ellie loved watching her older sister, Cathy, put on her makeup. Ellie wanted to wear makeup, too, but her mom said Ellie was too young. She could start to wear makeup when she turned Cathy's age.

Ellie thought this was unfair. She wanted to wear makeup right now. Ellie's mom told her that when she did get to wear makeup, it would be so exciting and worth the wait. Ellie felt better knowing that one day she would get to wear pretty makeup, too.

Ellie is sad because she is too young to wear makeup righ now, but her mom tells her she has something fun to ▶ look forward to when she is a little older.

How Older Siblings Can Help

Older siblings can be helpful. They can tell you what to expect on your first day of school. They can help you with your schoolwork and show you how to play a new game. Older siblings are also great for giving advice about how to solve a problem. You can learn a lot from their **experience**. Your older siblings will go through important and special events before you. When it's your turn, you will have a great **audience** to cheer you on.

◀ *You can learn a lot from your older siblings. They can also teach you how to play fun games.*

Batter Up!

When Danny saw his older brothers, Alfred and Andy, playing baseball, he wanted to join in the game. Only Danny didn't know how to play. Later that day, Alfred and Andy taught Danny how to catch the ball. They also showed him how to hit the ball with the bat. Alfred threw Danny the ball many times. Suddenly, Danny made a hit! Danny was so happy. Alfred and Andy were great brothers to help him learn how to play baseball.

When it's Danny's turn up at bat, his older brothers cheer him on. ▶

Listen to Me!

Do you ever feel that no one is listening to you at the dinner table? Maybe everyone else talks more often than you do? Sometimes your siblings might even speak more loudly. In a big family, there might be **competition** to speak. If you are having trouble getting a chance to say something, you need to let your family know how you feel. They do want to listen to you. You can say, "I'd like a turn to talk now." Always remember that even the youngest person in the family has important things to say.

◀ *Everyone deserves a chance to speak. This girl needs to let her family know she has something to say.*

Family Time

If you come from a big family with lots of siblings, it is always good to have some special time alone with your parents. This will give you a chance to let them know how you are doing. Maybe something is bothering you and you need their advice. Maybe you want to tell them how you feel about your new teacher, or how your sister taught you a great new dance. Your parents will love spending time with you. Watching you grow into the special person they know you are is one of their greatest pleasures!

Glossary

argue (AR-gyoo) When people who don't agree about something get angry with each other.

audience (AW-dee-ints) A group of people that watches or listens to something.

competition (kom-peh-TIH-shun) When someone tries hard to get something that someone else wants too.

compromise (KOM-pruh-myz) When people work out an argument by each giving in a little.

difficult (DIH-fuh-kult) Hard to deal with.

experience (ik-SPEER-ee-ents) An event in someone's life.

frustrating (FRUS-trayt-ing) When not being able to change a situation makes you feel angry or sad.

sibling (SIH-bling) A person's sister or brother.

Index